S0-FQY-371

About ERASING THE LINES:

Ray Greenblatt is more than a poet, he is a verbal photographer and film maker. Often his scenes are as clear and as sharp as those of Ansel Adams: all shadows and light, the raw beauty sucking the breath from your lungs. Sometimes they are images of Salvador Dali; life turned on its ear, as he exploits the irony of everyday life and everyday situations. He knows that memories do not unfold in a logical chain of events, each piece in chronological order, as a perfect vision. They unfold in our heads the way we actually see them, colored by our emotional and psychological reactions. He knows that the brain does not recall things like a camera, and each time we envision a scene or a memory, our vision changes. He constructs his poems the way our mind allows us to remember life, past events and memories take on a hint of the surreal, of the macabre.

Eileen D'Angelo, *Editor of Mad Poets Review*

Ray Greenblatt's poems bring in a vast wealth of culture-Irish, Hindu and Greek myths abound-yet the work itself has a built-in divining-rod for the raw, barely articulated edge that charges the lively imagination. His poems reach out to a part of the reader that is unschooled, unmapped-a great interior continent where the mysterious is commonplace and where the great voices start. And he takes you there with confidence and with a voice like a reed in the wind, the voice of a single man who confronts and richly names what's lost, found and longed for in our modern times.

Bill Van Buskirk, *Professor at LaSalle University*

Ray Greenblatt, a much published and sought-after reader, brings his own distinctive ear to the subtleties of nature. A lover of country trails and an observer along the seashore, Ray says stop and listen to the accent of things, to the distinctiveness of the world around you. He never ceases to keep his ear tuned to the nuances of the outdoors and embodies the eternal poet's quest to appreciate the now, the zen of the moment. With Ray you feel the mist in your face, the waves lapping along the seashore, and the glow of Andromeda. Poet of landscapes, Ray has poems too of inscapes; his love poems stay with you at times reminding the reader of the outstanding love lyrics of Kenneth Rexroth. Ray says join me. Let's take a walk. Let's stop and listen. There is much to value here.

Peter Krok, *Editor of Schuylkill Valley Journal*

# ERASING THE LINES

## POEMS BY

## RAY GREENBLATT

Copyright © 2006 by Ray Greenblatt

*All rights reserved. No part of this book shall be reproduced or transmitted in any form or by any means, electronic, mechanical, magnetic, photographic including photocopying, recording or by any information storage and retrieval system, without prior written permission of the publisher. No patent liability is assumed with respect to the use of the information contained herein. Although every precaution has been taken in the preparation of this book, the publisher and author assume no responsibility for errors or omissions. Neither is any liability assumed for damages resulting from the use of the information contained herein.*

ISBN 0-7414-3020-7


*Published by:*

**INFIのITY**
PUBLISHING.COM

*1094 New DeHaven Street, Suite 100*
*West Conshohocken, PA 19428-2713*
*Info@buybooksontheweb.com*
*www.buybooksontheweb.com*
*Toll-free (877) BUY BOOK*
*Local Phone (610) 941-9999*
*Fax (610) 941-9959*

*Printed in the United States of America*

*Printed on Recycled Paper*

*Published February 2006*

# TABLE OF CONTENTS

Acknowledgement is made to the following publications in which some of these poems first appeared:

Alpha Beat
Advocate
Bucks County Writer
Cecil County Maryland Annual Poetry Contest
Drexel Online Journal
Edgz
Edison Literary Review
Endicott Review
Erete's Bloom
Flesh From Ashes
Laughing Dog
Mad Poets Review
Mobius
Moon Reader
Newport This Week
Philadelphia Poets
Red Owl
River King
Ruah
Space & Time
The Moon
Village Rambler

*Special thanks go to Jeong-Hwan Kook, Romane Paul, Krista Peterson, and John Washington.*

# THE BLITZ

I'm driving
I've got to be there on time—
then it strikes
a fresh phrase
where did it come from?
a passing scene
an old memory dredged up
the present gnawing of a momentary problem
who knows?
now it starts to accrete
two images glued together
now forming into lines
a stanza emerges out of mental mist—
this looks interesting
like a ripe fruit growing clearer before me—
should I pull over?
but I'll be late
should I try to write while driving?
too dangerous—
I need a tape recorder!
no—no—think—
use that ancient art—memorization
say it over and over
it's getting stronger—
stay silent
don't turn on the radio
don't look out the window
or other ideas might rise—
memorize—memorize
and keep going!

## ON CLIMBING THE STAIRS
## TO THE AMPHITHEATER
## IN THE ACADEMY OF MUSIC

At the side entrance why
are they renting hiking boots?
Why did the ticket seller bless us?
We begin.
A young woman
a few steps ahead
paces us
then becomes a blip
in hyperspace.
On the second level of Purgatorio
we hear through an open door
brass practicing.
On the third level
when we hear woodwinds
I stick my head through the open door
to see a corridor leading
to what seems to be merely a restroom.
We continue.
A couple of men
a few years older than we
pass bragging something about
"workouts pay off."
Out of the corner of an eye
I glimpse Alpine sheep.
So much time gasps by.
Until we finally reach
the top floor.
My wife's Italian tan
turns to Celtic fire.
Yet she jabs me and leers
toward a ladder which points
to a trapdoor in the ceiling
and the roof
and heaven beyond.

## ON HIGH

(above Kensington Gardens)


Way up here
where the doves pullulate
the banners snap to
the winds congregate
where the rains decide
rare stars scintillate
spires duel the damp clouds
among chimneys crenellate,
people far below
are just no more than
inexplicable events.

We sit by the window which
holds light like an empty tumbler
wisely sipping drinks
passing judgments on
the Prince Albert Memorial
thinking we can hear
patriotic songs winding
out of the Royal Albert Hall,
as Round Pond adjusts
its monocle and squints
up at us.

# PHOTOS

Something had shifted in you
something had given.
You took me by the hand
and led me into the woods.
Though it was a bright
summer's day and warm
it seemed the sky was black
leaves on trees and mosses gray
(no, I insist this was not a dream).
You may take the photos,
you said
just tell me how I should pose.
Yet you seemed almost bored.
I asked if you
would take off your clothes
(we both knew I had wanted you to).

You did
with just a touch of shyness
it was mostly, I guess
the awkwardness of where to put your clothes
the discomfort of how to pose.
I was in ecstasy
I was numb with all kinds of desire
as you slouched there waiting
for my technicalities to be arranged.
Your coloring was tawny
moister clung to your skin
you were truly what creators
dream of in the woods
(I swear to you I'm telling the truth).
Then guilt rose as my gorge
was this a way to keep me
was this the way to let me go
were you feeling a new eroticism.

I arranged and rearranged you like a feast
I danced around you like a shaman
forever in the dark woods
with rare moments made from shafts of light.
Then distant voices were heard
you gathered up your fallen coverings
and like a stricken wild thing
were gone.
The photos turned out as dark
as withered rose petals.
You asked to have them all
then things between us never were the same.
Many years later I cannot remember
individual pictures I took of you
only a memory of a girl
and boy in lovely woods fast fading.

# ON THE WAY TO SOMEWHERE

In an unknown town
we sat in an elegant dining room
of an old hotel,
marble floor, paneled walls, lofty ceiling,
fine table settings
and a glowing candle at each one.
       Better inside than out.
       Dirt and blowing newspapers,
       mercurial squalls,
       a poor person angling down the street
       only one but others sure to follow.
Our grinning waiter said
we were his first customers,
last night only one.
My wife shook her head in disbelief.
       An automated baby grand was playing
       tunes from the swing era,
       invisible fingers pushing down keys
       much in the style my father played.
       It even took breaks between sets
       and I could imagine
       a cigarette in the air
       flicked by a portly ghost.
In the bathroom at home at four a. m.
a cool breeze wafting
I wonder if it was just a dream
rife with Freudian symbols.
And yet all we have is the past,
each present minute dying.
They say it's all in the striving,
but I've started to believe
it's about being there
then willing to look back.

## SIBELIUS' VIOLIN CONCERTO

Midori comes onstage
bringing meadows in her gown,
hair braided and swirled up
like a delicate geisha.
Then she spreads her legs
digs feet into the floor
as a football center
about to snap the ball.
While the music sweeps along
a silver twinkling shoe
peeks out now and then
to see if all this
sound is possible.
Her naked arm appears
so tender but within
moves titanium.
The bow beats the thing
on her shoulder into crooning,
reaching crescendo
upon crescendo
until it would outsing
a hundred instruments.
Finally violin
merges with orchestra
to forge a masterwork.

# THE BOOKSELLER

Eugene,
I've been thinking of you a lot lately
though I did not know you well,
especially when a day grows gray
or I find the people around me
insipid, including the face in the mirror.
When I walked into the store
I knew you were there—
walking into a garlic garden.
Your hair was matted
your pot belly
on a fragile frame
a misplaced boulder.
The quotation for the week
was stenciled on your t-shirt,
eyes magnified in those lenses
like pinballs bouncing
all around with a million ideas.
Your store more an old house
was filled
all rooms floor to ceiling
with books.
Almost everyday there
you would have lived in it
if the law allowed—
what was your family life?

You a former engineer
finally seduced by one book too many
that engulfed your heart with
who knows
insight, tenderness, grace
can anyone say?
Eugene, I think of you a lot these days—
that damned belly of yours
was no laughing matter
though you har-harred about it,
then the cancer grew
and knew no bounds
you never said a word
until it stilled you.
      But now at your weakest, invisible
you keep me going, friend
and how many others
we'll never know.

# MIDDLECLASS HOUSE

You could say
this house is haunted
for it sits hollow
most of the day until
people return at dusk
with a tread of dust
and hardly a halloo.

They ingest a bit of food
which becomes something else
flit through a newspaper
crumbling into vapor
strands of organ music
meanings only whispered.

Invisible pipes rush water
for a few life-like moments
then silence as sleepers
drift into another
ghostly realm.

## IT'S A LIVING

In a typical block
of shore town bungalows
a man sits at kitchen
table doing the accounts
in t-shirt, paunch drooping,
lion's roar of vacuum
muffled somewhere upstairs.
He has followed the music
from the Apple to Chi,
K.C. back to Motor
City even a while
down deep in Miami.

In an hour or so he sits
in tux in casino light
colored and powdered and bright
as any sun's attempt.
It's not the slick management
not the frenetic slots
not the paycheck for now,
but blowing in unison
with three other gleaming horns
getting a solo then and again
where his riff can take him
beyond the silver
beyond the clapping
beyond the sun.

## MOONFUL

Moonlight pours through the skylight
piling up pails deep
painting walls with Dover chalk
bathroom floor in faux snow.

We play at statues
holding outlandish poses
imagining alabaster,
flick white terry cloth
like ghostly toreadors,
chase each other
dough children who want to munch.

Now I know what B. Franklin
felt seated pudgy
in an empty bath tin
churning and chortling
as suds of thoughts flew.

OFFROAD

A poet cannot stand
the geometry
of expressways
no matter the straightness
of solid lines nor
the hypnotic dotted.

His vision wanders
to the shoulder where
shunned creatures hide in
the undergrowth or
it sweeps up to a passing
window to witness

an unusual act.
He breaks the golden mean
as he collects provisions
for the journey.

## DOWN SOUTH STREET

Amble down the narrow cobbled street
through depression 30's
Lost 20's
The Victorian Age
a Federalist Era
until you've arrived...

      dark brothers
      in suits & ties
      slide by in tinted SUV's

past flicks
      where man & woman
reveal more than nakedness
      sticking digits here & there
as if they've discovered
      the progenitor of the hot dog...

past a head shop
      where the occupants
      are so far off the ground
they view an aerial of
      Baghdad Baku Samarkand
they communicate mutely
      with Sinbad also sailing
      with Alibaba
            and his forty alter images...

      a bent figure scurries by
      kaftan billowing
      vellum unidentified underarm

old bikers gathered on the pavement
        chains clank & tink
a biker loves the smell of gas
        all kinds of gases
                diesel to Pennzoil
soon he too will be soaring
but on solid highway west
        into eternally setting sun
        100 miles at
                100 miles per hour
ignoring bloated cactuses
        jagged stone pinnacles
                his destination the wind…


these times are altering
these times can be precipitous

who's to say the girl
        in the alley
puking in the gangrened can
        her tattooed navel
                seeing more than she
        will not be more lucid
                tomorrow…


meanwhile, bunched in a corner
in a caffeine café
a middle-aged couple
she cuddling a pregnant midriff
with smug countenance
he patting a bald spot
now & again to see
if the bat has returned
order an Ultra Mocha for him
a Hyson Nippon for her
and continue to work at
unraveling the latest knot.

# FINAL PASSAGE

This is the Norwalk
dredged from the depths
nearly whole.
Emerald warm water
then saber gray and ice
elevator express
to Tartarus.
Was the sound that of
mountaintops ripping off,
did the captain think of tea?
The wheelhouse became
an aquarium
the fishes staring in.
Did humans sprout gills
flit off to find a meaning
their spirits in the coral.

## SMOKING IN THE RAIN

## AT EVERGREEN HOUSE

Where in this bloody county
can you smoke without
offending someone!
I sit under my umbrella
on old broken brick steps
my pipesmoke merging
with the rising mist.
Secretive squirrels
and erratic rabbits
are doing whatever they do
on twilight lawns.
Feeble fountains trickle up
water that is no match for
rain trickling down.
The musicologist's words ooze
out of open windows,
in loose widening loops.
Soon the music will escape
in long plumes dividing
into a polyphony of
branches which will
decorate these tired lonely trees.
My pipe playing over
rain not restraining its tone
I shake the umbrella
creak to my feet and go
into the chamber.

# CALIFORNIA RUNNING OVER

Under warm rain I skidded
down into the arroyo
to gape at the creek overflowing.
Except for sandals
I hunkered naked
and stared into noon.
Water worked its way into roots
of hair and made my brain tingle,
water coursed off my back
like rain off a shed roof,
or water running
just like in this stream.

The creek usually limp and shallow
now flexed and frothed
so that I hardly could believe.
Bits of fools' gold
tumbled by,
a cluster of grapes
still fast to its twig,
anything I could imagine
seemed to accrete in the flow.
I plunged in an arm
and pulled out a Costanoan
grandmother, plunged in an arm
to pull out a black foal
plunged in to discover
a vellum treaty.

I paused to swerve around,
pant at cool hills
so green for now.
I could feel that up the mountain
in forest thickness
eyes of bear wolf
cougar fox were on me
and I prayed the fat of the land
would stay just a little longer.

## LAST LESSON

To the old man on the porch
the lawn grew a white fence of Queen Anne's lace
with dense marshgrass beyond,
now and then the teasing enticement
of half-hidden glints of water.

He could see the baby of himself
playing on the grass
oblivious to brilliant sunlight,
his mouth a maw for all things green
even sand and a stray pebble.

Now predominant
was the acrid taste of a pill
on the back of his tongue
or the image of reeds clutched by ice
unless wind chose to bend them.

No, he no longer wanted
the ignorance of a child,
not the tortuous phase of middleage
too many mistakes
too much pain mixed with bliss.

But he had survived,
a quietness is what he sought
and sufficient stamina
to remember, to catch those many thoughts
like moths wild in the light

and change them into words
one art out of all human attempts
that he found gave meaning
to uncertainty,
depletion, time.

EVENING AT KUERNERS,

by Andrew Wyeth


I step into the painting
and follow you around.
Border trees on green-black hills.
Serpentine stone walls.
A hemlock shading the porch.
Moon out of sight
but whitening sky,
clouds, creek below the house.
The pond now dry
will one day fill again.

I've been here
as real as when you were here.
Though in different perspective,
slightly altered shapes
I recognize them all.
You sit on a bench
in front of the stove
drinking hard cider.
Before your eyes
Anna becomes a ghost
disappearing time and again.
You see the hooks
in the attic ceiling.
You watch the sick light
burning on the first floor.

Sometimes I feel my past
was lived, written, painted
by someone else
on ancient vellum.
You are just down the road
living your present life
second by second.
But one day this writing
will be a history of
a history of a history....

# WAITING FOR THE RIVER

The river has a secret
and I want to know it

      I know it started
      in a shaggy mountain
      birthed out of an icy pool

            that it can change shapes
            deep and narrowly sly
            or shallow fat in the sun

            men tried to chum it from a bridge
            catch it in a dam
            churn it with a mill

      but the river always makes it
      wondrously so in this marsh
      I am hiding to wait

for it to speak as
it gives up its last drops.

## CALLING FROM THE HILLS

I am calling you from the hills
I know you are caught in a skein of work
but I am confident
I will keep calling to you
until you come
until in the middle of a blue night
you will wake knowing
this is no worker's migraine
but a pure call of love
I have set up camp
near a stream that actually warbles
I don't know how
yet it tumbles out of the earth's source
joyous and singing
flowers I don't know yet
being a displaced Easterner
are generous with their odors
bold and startling with their colors
we will watch as fog settles
over the dusk
then as mist lifts at dawn
the sun will massage us
the chill will inspire us
we will share from a dented tin cup
we both love
which has traveled with us
on so many camping trips
come soon my love
I am waiting
practicing my patience
lengthening it until it becomes a gift
the aspen bending over our tent
will officiate.

## ON THE JOURNEY

Toward the end
of the journey
sand swirls into eyes
sun glare absolute,
one sharped string being
played eternally;

less hearing no sight
yet feeling is acute,
coldness in feet to
the open-windowed
doorless rooms in the head;

atlases useless
guidebooks outdated,
knees are final
transportation.

## WINTER COAST

I'm good for about ten minutes
on this morning walk
the bay chunked with ice
like pockets of anger

this time of year
we turn away from it
with a jab of fear
somewhere deep inside us

among its shades of gray
which encompass sky too
only a modern moralist
might find some pleasure

the town still lies comatose
a cough around the corner
a cat twice normal length
oozing across a yard

glance down a side street
there's always a "catfish row"
the "needy box" in the post office
is meant to deal with that

in the cemetery
with an indifferent wind
blowing over, what do
the dead think of honor

through the walls of a house
classical music seeping
like fragrant coffee
and I'm home.

## SMALL IRELAND?

You can't easily write
a short poem about Ireland,
the sky over it is too large
the sea it hovers in too vast
the famines, the treacheries
the heartaches particular to just one person
turn smallness into paradox
expanding it to include all.
       Gray sky green sward
I wear like a band
round my head each day.
Hedgerows, tinkers, peat smoke
stone fence posts
Soay sheep so similar to goats,
on a hill
boulder and cow stand together.
       You hear just beyond the gatepost:
"Do what I tell you or the giant of McGillicuddy Reeks
will get you."

Every foot of land has been lived
I dare not move
for fear of stepping
on a holy skull
a rare potsherd
a relic which might cure insomnia.
       Mist blows through the courtyard,
not rain—if it were rain
prospects would be horrifying—
just mist, like fragments of memories
down from the old mountain,
or clutches of ghosts
up from sacred lowground,
standing stones, holy trees, magic wells
desolate cottages, deserted chapels. . . . .

Even villages have alleys:
one always leads to the coal yard
and down another an old man lumbers
wearing his tweed coat
like a rhino wears his skin.

# SKYSCRAPERS

Skyscrapers are beyond my imagination!

They are not merely Olympians
but the generation of Titans and beyond.
These skyscrapers are truly Babels,
they will reach the heavens
because they are built on godless foundations,
blasphemous in their method of fabrication.
These colossal poles invade clouds
turning the sky eternally gray,
their nightly lights not beacons
instead inward souls scheming.

No!
lay then down
like so many conduits,
inside them let Superman race a projectile
until it exhausts itself
somewhere west of Ohio.
Let nomads erect brightly-colored tents inside
for all the horses of the Plains to be herded in.

Subways and tunnels are
the offspring of skyscrapers
piercing beneath Herculean waters
yet supporting them,
shafts to an underworld
where skyscraper morality lurks.
Watch out, China!

## FOG IN NEWPORT

The fog means business tonight.
It has already eaten
the harbor, the boats,
people in the dockside bars.
Foghorns seem nervous.
The fog rolls up streets
staining lights yellow
turning peeling clapboards
into a school girl's complexion
for the night.
An old man sticks his nose
out a window into the fog
as if it were chowder.
Soon the music chunking
above from a second floor
and from beneath a manhole cover
will be gone.
Fog dampens the sheets
and curdles your dreams.

# NEAR VALLEY FORGE

Stuck again in traffic
and it's raining.
The lines of vehicles
like a baggage train.
On the shoulder
goldenrod turning old
and new-turned milkweed
wave grimly.
A rusted muffler
resembling a defunct groundhog.
The truck in front
is a moving wall
obscuring all forward vision,
its bumper dripping
like a thawing bridge.
Then
a man with a musket lopes by
someone on a horse passes
a bullock cart grumbles past.
The corporate centers
grow wood plank sidings.
Mist kicked up by tires
which print maps in the wetness
mixes with campfire smoke.
And I wonder which battle
I'm better off fighting.

# NOCHE DE LOS MUERTOS RESTAURANT

From the ceramic tree
hang white skull
and bright fruit
pineapples, cherries, shells

     a waitress arrives
     with brimming drinks
     on the back of her hands
     flips them neatly over
     and delivers

in the tree of hollows
skeletons dance
playing fiddles and guitars
cigarettes in their mandibles
bow ties round their gullets

     three ladies
     at a corner table
     harmonize a brief
     song to themselves

the dead in the bush
wear top hats and kerchiefs
rainbow flowers
with broken pitchers
and a bull looking on

     a waiter carries
     a full tea service
     on his head, no hands
     pours cup after cup
     spoons tinkling like knives.

## THOSE WHO WAIT

We who wait honor you.
You are courageous
to wrestle living things
from tumultuous depths.
You are full of spirit
simply hoping for a wind
to catch sail and carry you away,
to what you never know
often until it's too late.
You are trustworthy, industrious, honorable. . . .
But we have not been
completely honest with you.
We have not revealed all.
We who wait
now remove the black shawl,
pull down the mask of
a withered old woman
glass beads of tears sewn on
mouth of agony punched through.
We have turned away from the dock
to prepare extravagant meals.
We have sung and danced
drunkenly in living rooms
like sorority girls again,
like working women on that two-
week vacation at the shore.
And too, the old men waiting with us
have regained new vitality.

We have gossiped over palings,
almost forgetting what lies
beyond the changing tides.
Trees sigh and seethe and roar
in fresh winds.
Squawking of fledglings in
the boathouse has continued
for hundreds of years.
We have not forgotten,
but we too must live in our way
as the world despite us rolls on.

# IN THE GREEN ZONE

A grove of trees
is allowed to live
between developments.

This is where green
becomes a living color.

This is where comix
are stashed till they rot.

This is where monsters dream
and are dreamed of.

This is where golden person
meets beige.

This is the initiation
of blood rites
with a mistossed stone.

This is where
a bare ass is first shown.

This is where the mores
of civilization are forged
and known.

COVER UP

You stand naked
in the shadows of the room

and people put up convertible tops
        in warm summer rain
and carpet hardwood floors
        with wall-to-wall shag
and my aunt covers every piece of furniture
        in her living room with transparent plastic
and a macho guy never feels pain
        never backs down, never cries
        and professors are never wrong
        and your lawyer sits down with you
        to tell you that he knew quite awhile ago
        that we were going to lose your case
        but he has another idea
and too many politicians just use words
        as decoration

and you walk out of the shadows straight towards me
and you're naked
and you don't care
and I don't care
and you look good!

# NEAR WINDOW ROCK

I'm standing at this school bus stop
in the middle of nowhere
like a fool
trying to imagine
what Indian kids see.
Do they hear the seething of silence?
Are those distant mountains
monsters or saviors to them?
When they first catch sight of the bus
is it as their ancestors
first glimpsed the gleam of armor.
Do they follow the patience
of the desert or like us
in a long slow line
of cars or customers
blow out of control.
Perhaps they see nothing
feel little now
whether solid heat or snow
raised on impoverishment
raised with humiliation.
My car is waiting
to get me out of here
but I'll bet this is
where they want to be.

# SEARCHING THROUGH THE MUSEUM

I haven't been in this museum for many
years but I know you're in there somewhere; how to hide,
who would dare destroy such primitive power.
I sit in the court by the fountain
reading to refresh myself on all your details,
then I enter the place that once was dark and as
eerie as the very tomb in which you were found.
I wander past Incan quipus, their strands and knots
unreadable, a totem pole that could become
a circus dancing beneath a midnight moon,
and photos of Polynesians who slew their flawed
children to continue their carefree perfection;
until I discover a huge new addition
filled with auditoriums, shops, and restaurants
that have made this place into something alien.
Finally in the rotunda I see you
as bold and blinding as my young eyes remembered;
your eyes are black jewels, your sword a silver wand,
your lacquered layers hiding a relic inside.
Will anyone in years from now look for our remains
as diligently and find them with such awe.

# HALF-STATES

(1)
In dream state
I hover above the bed
like a living tapestry
then foreshorten
or elongate into contours
of the hills
daring tortuous treks
recognizing in mountaincrest
three juggling balls
the moons of Saturn
greenhouse becoming city
streetcar strangers
incidental lovers
grandfathers
cards shuffled too quickly
until I curl unconsciously
into a warm sock.

(2)
Making love
is all senses at hazard—
lips persuasive speech—
crowds of lovers
in fingertips—
our conjunction bakes
and ululates—
flirting with the edge
of agony—
landscape of limbs—
cries mistaken
for ancient melodies—
lover's eyes
forged medallions
we hoard till time folds.

(3)

Yet I can lose myself
between bookends of thoughts.
I shamble through entranceways
of A then H
under the crooked lintel K.
The closets of my brain
are filled with pat phrases
never to be used again.
Rare times on parapet
I view the everlasting sea
and thunderous light,
before I dig once more
with pickaxe becoming pen.

# THE MYSTERY LOVER

Every poet has a mystery lover
sometimes so close to real
he sees it as through
the thinnest sheet of ice
a familiar face revealed.

Especially in far off places
where walking on strange streets
he looks at everyone
no matter how alien
as potentially known
an intimate composite.

Or on the sourest of days
when light does not appear
in sky or in one's soul
an unrealized lover
must be the only hope
that keeps him going.

Reality falls short over and over
and we must accept it
like holding a dull stone
but the poet gets to carving
to make something out of nothing.

## URBAN DRAMA

Tonight the city holds
                    the odor of bad breath.
Red fire hydrants lift legs
and trash bins flap wide green gums
                            as he passes.
In coffee bar windows
                    white-faced mannequins
                    with frizzed wigs
                    and black eye-sockets
                            turn toward him.


Then a blizzard
of dust and grit
            slices of paper
            with etched obscenities
                        ferry past.


Finally safe behind his apartment door
the silence feels icy
face in the mirror
        almost washed away
lights in buildings across the avenue
distant as Italian hill towns.
He punches in her long-distance number
and that voice at the end of one long filament
that voice with a history attached
        floods the rooms with heat.
He feels his muscles uncoiling
        lolls back in the chair. . .


when all lights wither to pinpoints
as a brown-out falls down on the city.

# WINTER FIELD

I trace two sides of that field
driving home from work,
the other two bordered
by trees which once, I imagine,
spread into forest;
I am terrified by it,
and elated.

After rain it reflects
its beauty in a sudden pond,
wears corsages of birds;
running through,
hieroglyphics of deer
in morning dew,
reciprocity of
earth and sky.

Come spring, will cornstalks rise there
like gleaming woods,
or a green sea of soy;
a farmhouse in the center
might be a jewel
in perfect setting.

But an infestation
of townhouses or
corporate center
or mall will drive nature underground
one more sad time;
and we know what happens
when man falls in love
with his own image.

# WATCH TIME: FOR 2005

The world is turning
slowly
     irrepressibly
         turning
a cosmic silver disc
on which are affixed
an actor
     stretched like a soaring staff
a singer
     mouth open
         as wide as a face
literary man
bent and windily white-haired
     slabs of tomes under each arm.

The world is turning
in a held silence
     as soft as snowdrop
before the modern
     flashings and roaring
     of a soon-to-arrive new year
tiny figures revolving on shadowed lawns
are goats   badgers   woodcocks
with humans clothed in cassocks
     so many humps in the landscape
who hold up candles whose tentative flames
     flicker with possibility
     with chance of extinguishment
chanting into tonight's last darkness.

## INTO PLOUGHSHARES

I will see your gun—
despite the valuable antique flintlock
hung over the walnut mantel
to pontificate on with brandy
those late dark nights
your toadies gathered about you,
or the graceful Webley-Vickers
snug under your armpit
contoured smoothly under any custom-made
pin-striped suit you might choose
from that long mustless closet—
I will see your gun only
as a toy in July
to fire for fun—
much like many dictators have done
standing proudly
on marble balconies—
to shoot a hot July
into an open-face sky.

I will play this shovel
this tool that has hidden
so many misdeeds
in shallow places encrusted
corroded with bone
and bits of skin—
I will play this shovel
like an iron drum
whose timbre has been overlooked
when only an odd pebble
half-heard the truth—
I will play iron upon iron
sparks of steel and tongue
until songs emerge from all tombs.

Even the axe
man's armor, man's offense
I will place it humbly
over the mantelpiece
now that all forests have been felled
all gaps have been bridged
all doors have been built oaken and yare—
we will breathe more easily
toasting its gleam, its perfected edge
with grapejuice and saltine
turning the datebook to see
if another year awaits us.

## WAITING FOR THE QE II

I'm waiting for the QE II
to steam up the river of this backwater port,
can you think of anything more exciting for us!
They'd see her coming down river
and the countryside would go wild,
screens of nervous birds rising and
calling across open spaces of marshland,
jeeps and cycles careering along shore roads
to bellow the news that our town
was host to a queen of the seas.

And then when she had arrived, smooth as a whale
panting next to our tiny pier,
deep deep horns breathing way down
through her funnels and shafts,
men in white sunhats puffing Cuban cheroots
would line rails and ladies in pastel frocks
would wave lace hankies, our village
children would dive off surrounding sailboats
(could they for once be naked and brown?)
yes, our children would dive for tossed coins
sparkling like firecrackers as they fell
to meet sparkling blue surf.

I know it's impossible, I know
our river is never anything but brown
that it's been silting up for the last two hundred years
but its long life deserves some kind of respect,
and as I come to die in this bed
which faces down river toward open sea
I'll still gasp as the huge white sides of her
like museums, stadiums, capitols gleaming in
afternoon sun, move past this window to cast
longer and longer shadows on my wall
until the moon out of embarrassment
will hide his head in clouds, then boldly show
tears on his face with the pride of it all.

## ACCEPTING SUMMER

We must accept summer
the sour sandy sheets
mildew behind the door
the awful absolute light
that fillets us
just as any fish
laying open its soul
on the scaling board;
when we slump in a chair
observing profusion
making no conclusion
until things change
until we alter;
we must wear summer's brand
and understand the panting
the blurred eyesight
till we gain insight;
we must learn summer
to know winter
then much more.

# VIEWING MARS

We climbed to the highest
window in the house
a loophole of glass in the attic.
Brushing away webs and dust
we glimpsed the planet,
a roaring gold
like a chip off the old moon
which had come up flushed orange
as if out of a saloon so long.
But this seeming boy
looking all the likeness
of a stalled plane,
posed there so bold
in his rare appearance.
Who this noon amidst the grainfields
pale as mist
could have imagined
such a day's longevity.

# LAND-LOCKED

We have a dozen words
for dust storms,
God's name is also
the name for oasis.
Our rocks are scrubbed clean,
many etched with dedications
to faceless persons.
We weep when we see
a yellow flower
growing among the stones,
we are awed at a gray
cloud passing over.
Our children dream of following narrow paths
for many blistering days
to an ocean
and there simply squatting in the sand
surrounded by bright-colored toys.
     They dream these reveries
over and over again, only
the music of the sea changing.
Our maidens, as well as widows,
pay dear prices for imported odd-shaped shells
they press against genitals
to fulfill secret wishes.
And our old men retell ancient tales
of galleons and pirates and scaly monsters
although often from awkward translaticns.
Out of our frustration, our desire
one brave soul would scale a pinnacle
as if it were a mast swaying
in the eternally static flatness,
until a mirage of tidal wave
took him smiling into its world.

## A WOMAN'S DESIRE

She had only one desire.

The vase sat in shadow
in a corner but would be
lovely near the window,
the renters would not
be back for weeks.

What else had she
to do but concentrate,
concentrate so hard
through the nights and days
in that sole chamber.

Until it moved--floated
slowly across the room
to lightly settle,
the silken blossoms
caressed by her transparent hands.

# THE SIGNING

I didn't want him
to sign the book,
just the page of that one poem
titled "Autumn."
When she first heard it years ago
she was struck.
I thought at first it was his voice,
but ever after she went back to it
that time of year.

My quest was ended.
Strange how I found him
in a restaurant
surrounded by noise and color.
Yet he seemed glad to do it
with a flourish and
I think a little smile.
He too is getting on.

Only a few months ago
it was nervous walking to nowhere,
now she sits blankly in her chair
perennials behind her she no longer sees.
Her hair was once a blaze of glory.
Chances are she won't even know
I don't know either,
I guess I wanted a kind of blessing
to let her know it's all right.

# MAN HOLE

It is the darkest secret,
I had to get away.
I clawed the dirt off
the half-buried lid
and levered it half-open.
Strange. Poe never thought of this,
and yet. . .
    The cover clanged shut
    with a surprising sound
    of purity, and I
    began to descend
    moist mossy rungs
    tearing through clotted webs
    that baptized my crisscrossed head,
    odors so fetid, so ancient,
    darkness so dense
    it pierced the eyes.
I shouted and the shout
coming back was no sound
like me, more like my younger
hopeful self or again,
a deluded older version.

And still I descend
joints worn, clacking
but now used to the climb
into a blind region.
And somehow I feel as if
I've entered myself
searching for god knows what
but I cannot stop.

# IN A CHINESE TEA HOUSE

Up in the hills above Hangzhou
we sat on wooden chairs
before an ebony table
in a wooden tea house.
Soft summer rain fell
on long rows of tea plants
whose leaves shed water
like tiny green roofs.
Our hostess poured tea into tiny cups,
the leaves flitting in circles
under the steaming waterfall
like a school of nervous fish in a pool.
        We sipped silently
feeling bucktoothed to strain
the liquid through numerous leaves
while she lectured on tea history.
A small tin box of tea
and a larger one sat before us
as she pointed out advantages
of buying more, this beautiful
undeterred teacher whose
clipped clear English filled
the hollow raftered room.
She left again
to let us think, we thought,
under the hissing roof.

Through slatted windows
a twitch of cloth in distant fields
told us pickers worked in the rain,
a metal bell clanged
dimly for unknown reasons.
Hostesses glided along balconies
outside the tea house complex
bearing trays of pots and boxes
and piles of green bills.
Time began to steep,
we looked at each other anxiously,
then the door opened again
and we bought the largest box
of the finest green tea
with sheepish smiles all around.

## FOR ROBERT FROST

I've had enough of the attic
I'm tired of the restive
noises at all hours
winters too static
summers too infernal
articles lost under eaves
places not safe to step
flying things keep intruding
memories jumbled with rubbish
I stand scratching my chalky skull
with chalky fingers
the closer to heaven
the angels speak too softly.

I now prefer the cellar
I've gotten used to more basic living
no heads to bump
it spreads in all directions
like an eternal boneyard
my history stacked in rows
so I know what I must
get rid of to move on
so what if water rises
I have boards to walk roughshod
dampen spirits but not my soul
close enough to interment
that I can thumb my nose.

# TWILIGHT CONVERSATION

While we stood talking
on the road as if
fate had intercepted us
you began to disappear.

Your face blurred
those striking eyes gone
the voice seeming to issue
from just a general distance.

All that remained of substance
was your words, the perfectly
reasoned sentences. But I
could only watch the white

the whiteness of your shirt
the whiteness of the paperback
you carried peeking out from
under your arm like a pet.

And then a sprinkling of stars
appeared behind you
in the pond framing
the presence that was not there.

# IN THE DELAWARE COUNTY SCIENCE MUSEUM (1868)

I gather with a group
                of ragtag magnificent poets
trudging in a rough circle
                on the old wooden floor.
We concentrate our psychic wherewithal
      focusing     focusing
         pulsing     pulsing
            praying....praying
almost tigers turning into butter
             in our attempts.
Suddenly
the antique glass cases begin to crack
to shatter in huge jagged flashing sheets
      with the jangling of cacophonous salutations.
All the birds in all their configurations
                 begin to flap

                      to rise,

our dedicated breath
      blowing away the dust on their backs
      the webs from their bellies.
They rise in a widening circle
        above our stunned wonder
in an instinctual gyre
        ever higher and higher,
carrying with them frogs on their backs
    like that Greek boy on a dolphin
    like Bellerophon on Pegasus
and snakes and squirrels and scorpions
    delicately in their talons
a gigantic circle of feathered life
    a kind of modern space ark
brushing gilt from the heavy rafters and cornices
            as they fly.

Then
the 21$^{st}$ Century
        with a hurricane of energy
       a cyclone of creativity
rips the roof off the building
         and the birds disperse
                  into the light.

Not to worry
nothing is lost of the past
archaeologists will have plenty to do.
The little boy on the sandlot
will scuff up a fossil to run home with,
and that girl pulling a brass telescope
out of the undergrowth
will stare through it at the heavens tonight
and glimpse a wondrous ring round the moon.

## NEAR SOUTHEASE ON THE RIVER OUSE
### (for Virginia Woolf)

The day was cold windy gray
the stones heavy in your pockets
your long black dress binding.
For the moment
you were a child
wading from bright beach
into warm surf.
Then you became something else
hidden intention suddenly blossomed
like trees that should not have been dying.
You sank as certain
as a goal for years labored.
Regardless of how you spoke
you could not bear
the voices anymore.
The body surfaced three weeks later
and with it
generations of newborn women
singing the century
as if they had stepped
like Aphrodite
out of the sea.

## VOODOO

How can there be hauntings
in the brilliance of sunlight.

Mostly bones
and a hank of hair
sits on the stone stoop of
an abandoned sugar mill.

Travelers climbing
what they thought a mountain
find flat mossy slabs
in perfect rectangles,
a bolt hole
now a black pool.

Down in town moonlight
crisscrosses a wall
like generations
of lashings.

The palms cast
longer shadows than themselves.
        The air is sown
        with flicks of blood.

## ON A COAST

I have never been here before
the wind is like no other I've known,

it cracks in over the sea
an arrow a lance a mile-long line
over the razorback waves
to snag us by the hair
making it stand like mindful runts
turning it to barbwire
freezing it into a new memory,

or catches us around the neck
as if saying this is the best damned place
no matter what your piddling biases
have convinced you of before
strangles us to confess
suffocates us into acceptance,

or loops around our waist
in an attempt at the erotic
as we might interpret it
without understanding any more
with no suggestion of empathy
only power sustaining power
that most likely will endure
beyond any soon squashed tenderness,

it ends in a subtle curl
a hard sharp flip
which comes back on us
behind us unexpectedly
with the added savor
of an odor we can't define. . . .

## TIGHTROPE WALKERS

In an ancient Italian town
by the sea
a group of daring acrobats
were performing high above the square.
They were short squat men who knew their art
twirling parti-colored parasols
wearing puffy clown clothes, riding cycles
juggling kitchenwares, then sitting
on chairs at a rickety table.

Our tumblers of Soave sat
before us but we could not move.
Then a woman dressed as a queen
in samite
began her journey from the shadowed
side of the square toward the bright
and I suddenly saw it was you.
Now halfway across that narrow wire
you paused and began to teeter.

I was almost out of my seat
and into the street to catch you
warmly clutch you to me in safety,
except instead you started to soar
up  up  up
your blond hair merging with the sun
your blue eyes becoming one with sky
your silver gown now a mere cloud
and I knew you had won success.

# PRESCRIPTION

O worker with a week's vacation
dare to go to a distant place

aged in your trade
without partner at home
go to a distant place for thrills

do not forget the thrills
like a nitro pill
intimately under the soft hot moist tongue

the pressure is so great
each mouthful must be
a little mound of gold—you must eat
sleeping in a perfectly soundless suite...

forget the sleep
open eyes wide
spin like a radar screen,
touch everything
slate rocks are keen
wooden boat hulls better,
and don't forget to inhale
most of us only do that
unconsciously these days,
you know voices quite well
listen to wind
a strange new language

but your time is darkening
you should be exhausted—that's good
what you store up will be
blubber through a long winter

if you don't do these things
you will shrivel shrivel

the only honest opinion:
run along a sea wall
and leap off!

(with no guilt)

# SCYLLA & CHARYBDIS: THE MAINE COAST

All the long winter
buzzsaws of wind are
hurled from granite mountains
and barbaric tangles
of spiked forests toward
the sea—gray and green boulders
of liquid miles deep
heaving and smashing together
to hurtle the weather inland,
       and caught in between
       in a purgatorio of snow
       humans barely surviving
in bone and shell houses
rattling their terrible songs
as from an open grave,
no more than white scarecrows
performing their chores
of pick-up truck, cutting logs
feeding the chickens, knitting
as prayers for another spring
when they can grow again.

## THE WAY A HOUSE WANTS IT

In the middle of the night
a sound in the house.
Not a person,
nothing like the scritching
of paws in the wall,
nor is it in a room.
I picture a grayness
growing inside the walls,
haze overcoming each window.
And the house slowly contracts
until. . .
Every room is simply
gleaming clean floorboards,
cream-colored walls shining
in late afternoon sun.
No pictures of remembrance hung,
no more ghosts of humans
to clutter up the place.

# THE SUMMER WIND

A summer wind blows
in the sea and time
sweeps in smells of brine and truth
whirls in a current
to clothe us with degrees
odors of salt and straw
and roots and cedar,
no matter where you are
it makes each car a racer
makes figures glide through darkness
makes all women provocative
wearing thigh-high skirts
whether they do or not,
the wind plays with sounds
placing them there and here
keeps a beat going through the night
hint of a dog voice
is scraping of a shoe,
the wind turns every
building to roadhouse
offers a mug of wine
to all sad souls who can
dream about a tomorrow,
the trees lean over
to set a laurel on our brow.

# NEW ENGLAND HOUSE

I don't stumble into furniture anymore
in daytime or in dark
because I've cleared it all out.

Only natural light fills the rooms
light as cold as spindrift
I open doors to let stiff wind sweep up.

I used to go down to the shore
where sand was a golden fleece
now I can't even dig under its gray shroud
now the sea just screams.

Melville's Piazza Tales lies on the sill
pages flipping aimlessly.

Many times walking by
Andrew Wyeth has rearranged windows
yet he knows just the outside.

In the deepest dark
I've wrestled over a gun with Robert Frost.

The nursing home on the hill
is a lot like this one
nothing living
no more than flickering gaslight.

I've lied to you
it's only October First
I sleep in a bed in an upstairs backroom
vegetables still remain from the summer garden.

I'll soon head south to get back to work
but I'll go alone.

# IN THE CORVINE KINGDOM

They live in those lofty halls,
he said pointing up with his cane
at the huge old trees.
They are as impenetrable
as the stone bastions at your feet,
he inclined his head toward
the solid bridge on which
we were standing.
He snorted, you wouldn't know
this thick foliage
--as resilient as a wall--
hides the stream below,
and he slashed with his stick.
It pours wildly over
cataracts not far away.
Many unseen, unexplained
things abide here.
Those giant bees suspended
dead by gossamer threads
serve as warning.
If they see you coming
from even miles away
they will slip out and glide
like shadows down the mountainside
hovering over the valley.
Suddenly the trees as a body
began to tremble and groan.
You think it's just the wind?
he looked about carefully.
Their calls can be unsettling
or oh so soothing.

They will return at dusk
knowing that if you still remain
you are more susceptible
to their control—he paused,
do you hear that distant roar,
and that fluttering in the tower
of trees.  They are already
trying to test our defenses.

# FOUNDATIONS

Earth has won
at least for awhile.
Lots were oversold
now builders sit bankrupt.
Through the field curves a dusty road
but it is already evaporating
concrete curbs already cracking.
Batterboards where houses
might have reared are rotting
string twanging and spranging
over windy nights.
Phone lines
        gas pipes
               water mains
all lie underground in new entombment.
May slug and snake and rat
make sewers friendly habitat.
May mole and vole
hardy busy miners
nibble electric wires
to add mystical sparks
to wild asters and wolfbane.
And cut tv cables
which reproduce false visions of dreamland.
Reality has returned
at least for awhile.

# BIOGRAPHY

It happened in the first four pages.

He was a darkly handsome young man
who wanted to be an engineer.
She was petite, pretty and energetic
although poverty was all she had known.
I was for them.
I wanted them to succeed.

Then a darkness began to fall
across the pages.
She became pregnant
unwantedly.
Germany slid into another depression.
They named him Adolph.

I ripped out all the other pages
to stop that one life continuing,
but the fury of the act
let some escape out the window.

# FABRICATION

I wave my hands
in cobwebs of confusions
fabricating mysteries—
birds fly out
dits of tanager
dahs of finch
purple martins in grand ellipses.
I stomp my feet
in fine imitation
of dusty buffalo,
my squeakiest voice
is squeaky violin.
Then while I could only
see murder in all mirrors
out of my pen
as gentle as itself
a deer at dawn
taking the pond for granted
becoming a reed in the breeze.

# ASBURY PARK EPOCH

These men want no part of a hot beach
they could care less about a cold pool
they prefer the second floor porch
under the awning where they all bring
their bellies like sacks of provisions
their wives below in a cabana
building a palace of mah-jongg tiles.

One man wears a ball cap backwards
looking slightly akin to a yarmulke
another a touch of Old World facial hair
another shoulder hair draped as if a talus
they throw down their cards
sometimes like a bird freed
sometimes like a keen knife
a joke  an insight  a belch
they toast with goblets of Upstate beer
incense from fat Tampa cigars.

And as the years of many summers go by
and wind whistles through the holes
growing wider between the men
they are thankful for what they have
although their ancestors are all gone
they do not have numbers on their arms
and they can walk away from this game of chance
whenever they choose.

## CONDO ON THE COAST

Yes, the ocean is good at roaring
the rocks alive with umber and slate and russet
glaring fog fills the windows.

But these rooms feel so bland
so simply white and square
furnishings petite and static.
I try to fill at least one room
with an empty beer can or two
making rings on
an invisible glass table.
Then a large ashtray
piled with gray smudges.
An unfinished plate of food
a leaning tower of books
clothes tossed about
on model-thin chairs
on prim divans
facing each other
boxes of miscellany
spilling onto the rug—
But the innocuous sand-toned rug
firmly grasps everything
diminishes it
and places it.

I remain a stranger here
a captive
in this exclusive district.

# AT SEA

I wake to a brilliant sea
but to my terror
to my ultimate horror
it is all around me,
a green liquid earth heaving
the cataclysmic blueness of sky
enveloping me.

They warned me about
the sporadic breaking through of the tides
but nothing like this,
after having saved for a lifetime
to purchase this magic house
which has grown to symbolize my life.

Somewhere to the far north was a village
somewhere just south my pool
whose feeble waters ocean has reclaimed.

I spy dolphins and whales cavorting
among shadows of ghastly waves
and as the moon's half-eye scowls down
I hear a tremendous rending below me.

I will light every candle, every lantern
before this stricken ark is launched
so that safe dwellings on the new coast
will wonder if a liner approaches
or a ghost ship has risen from the deep.

# TRAIN

Perhaps the train is not eternal
as a river
nor as graceful,
but it follows a path
chugs along towing its episodes
hesitant on uphills
compromised on curves.
        The train resembles a house
you take with you
generation after generation—
dining room where a meal waits
as certain as any death,
bedroom where a pullman
swings like a tropical hammock,
parlor with so many plush sofas
pushed into intimacy.
Here you can't get away
as at a dance or in a bar
where side doors are handy.
        I remember the taste of ham & cheese
compressed between thin white
wrapped in cellophane
mixed with coal smoke—
always exotic and savory,
pushcarts sashaying the aisle
with candy and magazines,
conductors calling in foreign English.
So many scenes flick by,
until a blur like a cardshark's shuffle
until a conversation
turns a passenger inward.

What would Indians on the outside see
resting their ponies high on a butte—
an ugly puffing thing
certainly not the indomitable heart
and burning soul of buffalo,
but a string of misshapen tents
tied to a wooden trail going nowhere.
What did the Captains of Industry think
in their private cars
forced to play in miniature space,
tiny teacups in meathook grasp,
suspended over wriggling wc's.
　　　　But the train is dying out.
We're not speaking of essential runs—
the political connections
of the Trans-Siberian,
nor the economic ties
between Bombay and Calcutta.
The Orient Express swirled its last intrigue—
leather saturated with fragrance
of Turkish tobacco,
brass fittings smeared with grime,
a hundred years of ghosts reflected
in every glassed compartment.
　　　　Inching toward the edge of the world
the last Irish train glides over bogland
allowing magic trees and holy well
to take their rightful place again.
What can we hope for
to interconnect all continents—
a tunnel beneath the ocean
(the Chunnel works on smaller scale!),
somehow shrink a train
to fit through the Trans-Atlantic cable?

I am so proud in my shiny cordovans
taking my mother's mint-scented hand,
where two street people look up from a broken beach
at a shaft of wind
when our invisible train enters
the Great Urban Station,
its bells blending with the closing bell
heard through an open window of the Stock Exchange,
its horn I always mistake for a police car
hee-hawing down a Cold War Berlin boulevard.
Not until the train has surely stopped
do we step out regally
to find ourselves in Penney's Department Store.

## 1920's, PARIS

Few years ago I was running
with a fast crowd in Paris
not holding my liquor very well
going to a Montmartre club where
a fabulous jazz band played
way into the dawn and women
danced naked on tabletops, their trick
to pick up things without using hands.
Some nights when my fog had dwindled
to mere haze I'd stumble outside
to stand with the doorman ablaze
in his brass buttons and top hat,
rather tall handsome-looking man
mulatto but smart with gentle voice
who talked with me about many things;
he'd traveled much across the world
had been a steward on a train
well as pot scrubber to make ends meet.
Came to realize recently
that he had turned me around
had showed me life is worth living
so I returned home to try again;
I wonder where he is now
I'll never forget his name, Langston
I hope that he is faring well.

## BOOTH

I see you sitting there
pale face
drooping mustache
though I can see through you
I see you slumped in that chair
waiting for the hour.

It is time to do it again
to pull that trigger over and over
into eternity
to take the life of a man
the whole world loves
they loved him then
they loved him afterwards even more
as he grew into immortality
like you.

You are eons beyond
feeling guilt
admitting that guilt
pleading any sort of respite
for your immortal title
lies on the dark side of the moon
in the face of Janus in shadow.

# NAUSICAA

Nausicaa arrives
Nausicaa of the white skin
and the long legs
Nausicaa of the broad forehead
and the amethyst eyes.
We go for a swim in a high tide
she wearing strands of seaweed
swim with the oysters and bass
a diadem of birds against the sun.
At night over candlelight
in fluted tones as sweet as ripe fruit
she tells tales
of her narrow undulating island
where stone seals and heron
come to life on moonlit beach,
where birds of multi-colors
speak perched on her shoulder
to whisper sea secrets
and to straighten her windswept hair.
She tells of her ancient father
the gandy-legged one
who could predict weather
a thousand miles off
by chimes and tubes and hanging pots.
At dawn she is gone.

# EXPATRIATE

In the dark I stand
on top of the tropical mountain
waiting for a wind
I will strip off my clothes too
to make that wind the coldest possible,
but when it comes it feels tepid
sweat still tattooing my skin
not like cold steel from the North—
and nettles are searing my ankles.

I wait for prevailing westerlies
to carry in rain
pray sky will darken
as it does over black spruce mountains,
sitting in my chair by the window
I close my eyes tight till they tear
as the rain does on the louvres
imagine rain turns sleety
snow piles up around palm trees
while my eyes continue to tear.

I have given up looking for
brown leaves, falling leaves
something so simple.
Ocean is blinding blue
not moods of gray
not one shard of ice.

Of course I pump people
fresh off a plane for news
not strained through newspapers
but rough and chunky
from hot mouths and gnarled
imaginations—but it's not enough.

Only in the stifling small library
in the back of the second floor
of Government House
where few people go
and the one librarian nods
like a guard in the Metropolitan
am I able to transcend,
can I become Northern
for a few moments
surrounded by tall wooden bookshelves
slumped in a cracked green leather chair
smelling old books, turning pages
watching the life of a silverfish
move irrepressibly over paper
common to us all.

# ON A VENETIAN CANAL

Like riding on an oily snake
the gondola slurps and lisps through
tepid sooty water from the south
riffled by currents of wind from the north,
avoid discharges from a third floor chamber pot,
bright cloth hanging limply from balconies,
always the shadow of a priest in an alcove,
into the mouths of bridges then spewed out again
as quickly as a time warp,
pigeons filling the air like holey vestments,
odor of garbage and garlic,
cellars here are aquariums
where everyone's ancestor is a fish,
not on way to a cathedral
but to a square where at a tiny table
you sip espresso or campari
waiting for a burnished sunset
waiting to hear dead quartets of violins,
where the ancient statues nod
and bow and wave like ladies of the night.

## AMISH COUNTRY

On the sky the artist
flicks specks of india ink
which become birds wheeling
then they fill a stripped tree
with black blossoms. Here
a man still plows with a team
and carriages defy
the hard-topped highways.
In the inn where we warm
before an old fireplace
a drawing of a cow's skull
matches in worth a print
of farmboy in trousers
years too large smoking
a cigarette with a wink.
It is ugly as winter
gets but hushed colors
on the hills and fields
can still fill a spectrum.

## DEER BONES

When the brothers
found the skeleton
Abel took the skull home
to put it on his desk.
At first he thought he'd make
a clock but only time
would be counted. Then
he found a little injured
bird he gave a nest inside
the skull.
        Meanwhile, Cain had been
polishing a thigh bone and polishing
until his arms throbbed.
When given a chance he would
beat that bird into mush.

# IN SUMMER

In summer
you are not you.
You are a stained and
oiled board lying on the beach.
You become a sea creature
eyes as blankly blue
as sky or underneath.
You do not eat
you inhale the eel grass
the salted air.
You do not speak
you do not even think
as most of us know it.
When you move
it is with the wind
changing into the chill
of six o'clock shadows.
Your sense of time stretches
beyond hours or even days
into a continuum of suns.

## POETESS AT HER OWN RECEPTION

You shuffle in,
not glide with
white scarf flowing
carnation bulging in your buttonhole.
Your voice flutters,
not a freezing growl.
It's been ten years.
Your fingers quiver
on the bottle neck,
your glance flits past my face
dares not hold for long,
maybe stirred by me.
You hide beneath that bush of beard
perhaps a tiger's eyes behind dark leaves,
strange habitat to unfold.
Across the room you slouch
like a terra cotta statue
draped in oil rags.
Chance for a quickie
on the table in the back room
but it's heaped with books,
a lumpy excuse for a regal couch.
I must remind myself
I am the poetess
offering her wares
as delicately
as golden butterfly wings.
After all these years
you finger my book
as if you could snap my culottes.
Have you found page forty-two
where I tell what I want in a man
without the muse's mask.

# OUT IN THE COUNTRY

Out in the country
nothing is ever quite finished,
a pile of rocks
or a pile of logs,
an outbuilding of no use.
The pear trees glow in whiteness,
the cherries blow petals
away in any direction,
bright mustard covers fallow fields
which will soon change
to uniform green,
but plowing will begin.
It's as if they are saying
don't be fooled by
just pretty colors,
only a dislocated
poet (probably from the city)
would stand and moon.

# ERATOSTHENES IN THE LIBRARY AT ALEXANDRIA

I have lived the good life.
I have just had a refreshing walk
to our splendid lighthouse and back again,
to where I now sit in this library
of hundreds of thousands of books,
in the cool shadows of this building
which will last—must last for eternity.
What a delight to dabble in what I wish—
drama, history, mathematics, ethics.  .  .
I have traveled, studied and taught
in Rhodes as well as Athens.
Yes, life has been very kind.
But can a discovery be evil,
can truth no longer be beautiful?
Let me relate what is so disturbing.
On the summer solstice I measured that
the sun had a seven percent inclination.
Behold, a correspondent in Aswan
south from here five hundred miles
found the sun to be directly overhead.
             What can this evidence imply?
That the surface of the earth curves.
And to conclude my calculations,
I determined the circumference of
the entire world—twenty-five thousand miles.
That suggests.  .  . I dare not say,
as head librarian, as tutor
to King Ptolemy's son I dare not
shock our reputable world of philosophy.
But secretly in these shadows
where I feel safe for the moment
I can whisper what it all means
is that seventy-five percent
of the world lies yet undiscovered!

It would be quite difficult,
indeed, it would be pigheaded to believe
that all that unknown was mere water –
land lies out there, perhaps land
rich enough to rival our own!
Oh, I must calm myself or else
go blind with anxiety
as to what should be done.

# POINT OF SATURATION

A point of saturation is reached
when so much concrete is poured
along the coast of the sea.
As buildings rise and
cement smeared into streets
people turn inward
thinking of silken shirts,
porcelain cups, humming cars.
Trees whether palm or fir
are razed or fenced in
dusty local squares.
Their whirling flights unnoticed
wild sea birds become pigeons
ubiquitous beggars.
Even the rhythmic cosmic
roar of the tides is obscured
by motors and marching bands.
And our innate search for the hills
is thwarted so at dusk
a few ask themselves why
the melancholy staring
at fading gold on the sill.

## PICNIC IN A PARK

Come take a stroll,
sun glints off footstones
like a string of festival lights,
no bony hand will reach up
to snatch you—it's a bonny day,
headstones stick up
like fistfuls of gimcracks
sold at a carnival,
mausoleums no
more than cabanas,
a stone angel might
dance in the soft air,
spread out a bright blanket
dust off an ancient toppled marker
for an updated seat,
out of the wicker hamper
cut a slice of melon
uncap the cold beer,
let the talk be loud
the laughter be true,
the dead can still enjoy
your joy of living.

# PRIMAL

All night long
you have lain
in a strange trance
hearing the ocean all around,
it is a bewitching song
but a sound never found
even on Schoenberg's 12-tone scale.
You lay listening through the hours
trying to define the key,
but not all the vehicles
the buildings
the lights
the feats of Army engineers
could reassure you.
For deep within you
is a primal anxiety
an anxiety you once confronted,
you know this is magic ground
an Atlantis over and over again
no wonder animals who live here
only fly or swim.
You are infinitesimal
and have ultimate respect,
you are infinitesimal
and hold great fear.

## THE LAST WHIRL

We don't have much time
decorate the rooms once more
swathe the walls lemon
persimmon lime,
turn that CD thing
—twirl the dials till it works—
up loud so we can hear,
wear your most sparkling gown
as we glazed-eyes swirl around,
I'll grab your amplitude
as light as lenten stilts
suck those lips that sucked
a shadowed lengthy life,
I'll stick my nose deep into
the vase of roses for a whiff
until the thorns prick me alert,
then we'll sprawl panting on the couch
leafing through the albums
until dawn as if some foreign
firing squad were lined up and drawn.

# THE OCEAN CAME TO US TODAY

(9/19/03)

The ocean came to us today.

The hurricane inhaled the river
startling boats with brown-ribbed mud
beneath them then spewing out
a surge that sent them
through marina roofs.

Canoes sprung up on streets
like sea serpents' teeth sown,
whitecaps in the park
and distant growling suitable
only for leviathans.

People seldom seen before
were driven out of black backrooms
to perch uneasily on porches,
rare prayers for power
to be soon restored.

In this slow-moving town
we've been lulled by gentle lapping
of fresh water but now
a mixture of soil and brine
hangs heavily on the air.

We have jetsam on each house
to mark the highest reach
of that titanic salty tongue,
one day becoming historical
plaques for people to look askance.

The ocean came to us today.

# MOON OVER THE CITY

What do you see of nature
living in the city—
that moldy squirrel
some brownish blades of grass
or well-tamed planetree?

Let imaginings of
a moonlit night
wake you in a fever
to take you up to the roof
where I can proffer
a sip from a cup of moon.

The moon is a burning wick
like many urban candles,
indeed cities inhabit it.

And if you've given up on
that jellied thing called river
know moon and sun war over
its waters through eternity.

# POEM TO THE WORLD

I do not want to write
an impersonal poem,
bound forever in a volume
with cold words as its
only medium.
I want you to feel
as if you are here.

I want the real world
—this present day, this second—
to intrude.
Now, see how the sunlight
today's sunshine, has already
yellowed the edges of this page.

Notice the fine wrinkles made
by a teasing breeze.

A shadow now inches across
this sheet—I will crease
the upper right corner
just where the shadow falls—there!

It is a hot day
and I am sweating so
I will let fall a drop
in the midst of the lines.
(look for it!)

Yet with all this tinkering
to bring real life to the poem
it still remains somehow removed.

So I will take it onto the lawn
(the words on the page
resemble the general shape, and
proportions of my house to the yard)
then you put it down
to let sun, shadow, wind
name it, let dampness, rain, time
claim it till they become one.

# About the Author

Ray Greenblatt has been an English teacher for forty years at The Church Farm School in Paoli, Pennsylvania. During that time he has had his poetry published in a variety of periodicals across America as well as in Canada, Ireland, and Italy. His work was also translated into Polish and Japanese. He has been nominated twice for the Pushcart Prize. He was a winner of the Mad Poets Annual Contest and the Anthony Byrne Prize for Poetry sponsored by the Irish Edition and Trinity College, Dublin.